Dare To Love

A poetic adventure about embracing
soul level freedom and discovering inner
self-love.

Written by Gina Louise Della Valle

Illustrated by Marisa Camille Berkey

Alex "Uncle Al" Della Valle, 1978
Oil on Canvas

Thank you to all who inspire my writing, listen to my dreams, and see my heart.

Much love,
GDV

Made in the USA
Atlanta, Georgia
25 April 2021
Scorpio Full Moon

Special Acknowledgments

To my parents, Cindy and Phil, for always allowing me to dream. Thank you for raising me to have faith in things I cannot see. Your love breaks the boundaries of space and time.

*To my brothers, Nick and Jesse, for always including me.
Thank you for coming to my 4th grade basketball games and telling me good job even when I shot the ball in the other team's hoop.*

To my late Uncle Al, who's spirit lives on within me and helps me connect to my creative nature. Thank you for your beautiful color you gave to the world, and the painting on this cover from 1978.

To my late grandma Angela, who was a true Queen and a fighting Angel. Thank you for coming with me in spirit to Atlanta, just after you passed. Your spirit has been my guide and your jewelery has been my armor.

To my late Pa, for always reminding me to dance in the yard. You were a solider of structure and family values.

To my late Gida, for always reminding me to "Go with God" and look to the sky. You were a strong and stood your ground.

To Carly, Amanda, and my beautiful cousins & aunts. Thank you for reminding me what it means to be simple, stable, and kind. Thank you for showing me what it means to listen with love.

To my close friends, thank you for your support and patience as I change my mind one thousand times a day. You all make me feel safe and secure to be Gina.

*To my school students, especially those who cannot speak.
We have talked more than some people with audible voices ever will.*

& lastly, to my other half that showed me my whole within <3

I love you all.

Contents...

Contents continued...

~About the Author & Illustrator

Introduction:
What is the Divine?

Everyone is born, and everyone will die.
These are the truths that we can all agree on.
We are all born divine.
Born without a built-up ego, with no conditioning, no awareness of social
norms, no judgments, and no deep-rooted animosities towards others.
Born without a broken heart, without shame, without guilt, and without strict
obligations.

The question I began to ask myself is, *how do I access my divine state?*
The state some people sense when they hold a newborn baby.
The state some people feel when they fall in love, overwhelmed by the purity of
creation and joy.
I want to find it, and I want to live in that state.

We are all Queens. We are also all Kings.

What have we learned from our history books about Queens?
They are protected, cared for, and watched over.
They have an army of suitors, and people who want to care for them.
Queens must remain sacred, must be protected, and must never enter harms
way.
Queens want to serve the collective.
Queens want to bring people together through love.

But what happens when the Queen wants to be the one to protect?
...When the Queen wants to stand and speak without a script?
...When the Queen's protectors have done their part, and now she can fully
serve?
She awakens.
She realizes she has a special mission to uplift and spread her love to all beings.

**These free-verse poems and visuals serve to link all souls with their own unique and
divine nature and remind us that we have all we need on the inside, if we just listen.**

Do. Not. Enter.

Don't. Do. Not. Enter.

Sir, please surrender.
Back down. Just rest.
Regress, at best.
The easy way to be.
Yet easy, I say, is not for me, today.

Being free comes at a cost.
It is not, just a thought.
Freedom is not, a jolly skipping trot.
Freedom is not, something that's bought.

Freedom in mind, body, spirit,
is what we all must be.
Why can we not hear it?
The cries of so many.

The bellows, the brawls.
The feelings we hide
behind barren eyes.

We don't listen
to the inner call
until the inner call
is
all
we
hear.
Till small talk falls on our deaf ears.

Do. Not. Enter.
This is what we tell our own soul.

Do. Not. Enter is wrong;
Right is, Do Not Fear.

Stargaze Beside Me

Some people
will do a lot for you.
But is that not
just the issue?

For *you.*

I want someone
to stargaze beside me
because
they want to.

There is something
to be said about
that equal silence
between two people
who are engaging
in something
that they are equally
passionate about.

Two people
who share a
common energy
out of passion
and
out of love.

Create the energy
you want for yourself
and attract those
who want
that
too.

New Year's Eve Mantra

Find peace within you.

It's a New Year,
time for changes and to embrace the unknown.
Time for myself to regain back my self-confidence
and to actively search
for it within.
Use those impulses and
light
it
on
fire.

Looking elsewhere
for what you already have.
Approval and feel-good words
won't feed your heart.
The feeling is not found in others
but deep in your own core
of your own being.

These pathways of
negativity
toxicity
victimization
must end
now.

Feel it for what it is
and
let
that
ish
go.

Spirals

I caught you
in your spirals
down your own
red wishing well.

Now I am circling too fast
down your own
red hissing hell.

At last, I see
a
red
rose.

I rise above
from your heart's
red missing cell.

Toxicity

Practice your patience
in front of a mirror.

"I don't like when you talk to me like that."
Stand up for yourself.
No one else will
if you don't
first.

Be stern.
Stand your ground.

Low self-esteem
is not for you
today.

The lost. The broken. The hateful.
Help build them up.
So they can stand, too.

Then you stand together
and see all things through.

Landscape of Plants

The vegetation around you
symbolizes
the vegetation of yourself.

Do you tend to
the leaves needs?

Do you water the leaves
with ease?

Do you tend to
your own
mental
physical
spiritual
feeds?

Observe your landscape.

Of White Sage

As I waved goodbye,
I felt a stillness in my heart.
A feeling of unknown
yet peace.
Everything that has led me
to this point
I owe to them.

I have the ability
to think, to live
for myself now.

I can go wherever, whenever.
I can trust my spirit.
I can make my mind still and calm.

I am embracing freedom today.
I am embracing peace of mind today.
I am encompassing compassion today
and a healthy sense of curiosity.

My heart is on fire.
like a stick of white sage
embers burning slow;
unhurried at a healthy age.

My love comes from them.
I can feel the love on my lips
tingling in the warm air
and in the cold air.
I envision my love as free air
through the thin smoke
as I wave goodbye
to the ones who care.

Africa Sober

What if we could freeze our soul
at its' most youthful state?

There will be a time for everything you want to do.

Your visions, how rosen
developing in cocoons.
Your life's passions and fleeting desires
only last a split second in your head
only glimpses of your dreams
like fires spreading without clear reason
through African plains in the arid season.

Your soul expands
but not yet awake,
still you check off "frozen" as your state of being.

Creativity interrupted
by nothing but your own angst.
No more aids, no vices.
Uncomfortably clear.
You have paid, made entices,
toward living in fog
because of the comfort
it applied to your heart.

Only to awake, and ache
abandoning the urge to do wrong
because now right is easier.

Shifting
Clearing
Sobering Soul.

Diving

grandma
angela

lips, ears
tingling

arms tingling

mirror
reflection

Faces/people

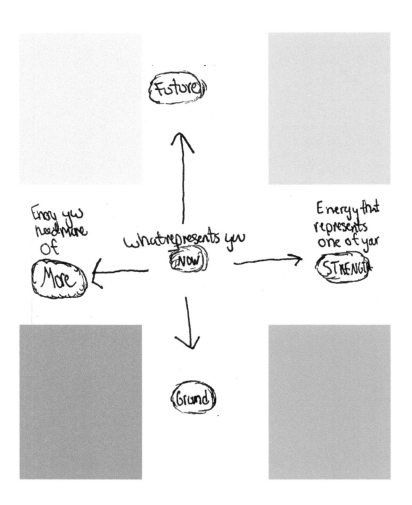

Future

Energy you need more of

More

What represents you NOW

Energy that represents one of your STRENGTH

Ground

Girl at Sea

What are you fishing for?
My higher purpose. My sense of Self.

I lost her. Her experiences in this body feel like a distant, barren land.
Running through the daily motions, as detached as a kangaroo is from land
upon the first high jump of the day. Detached as a New Moon passing
through Aquarius. What are you fishing for? My intuition. She tried to catch
me, but I did not listen. She gave up. She started to creep up and speak up,
channeling through other people. Some with rough hands, some with soft
hearts. Still, I did not listen. She would not take no for an answer. She would
push and push and push. Until my body finally felt the pressure. The pressure
to make a shift. To unleash back to my higher being, with love and an open
heart. What are you fishing for? Lost girl at sea? Is it acceptance, validation,
attention, lust, vulnerability, power, passion, affection, connection,
protection, security? Girl at sea, you are fishing with your own hook caught
on your kimono. What are you fishing for, girl at sea?
Watch your thoughts. Take your bait. What is within is what you are fishing
for.
So go. Go. Girl at sea. Go reel the line in. Reel it in, link that hook to your
heart. Pierce it, let the de-oxygenated blood rush out, feel the pain. Heal your
heart. The type of fish you want are not going to find you until you decide
where to throw your line. You have tampered so much out here. You hurled
your own body into the dark, deep waters with no regard for your oxygen-
craving soul. But you still radiate, even with your scars. You are still beauty.
The beauty that you will not give to your higher self but give to everyone else.
What are you fishing for, girl at sea? You were fishing for you all along. You
could not see you. So others had to show you yourself. Thank them for their
help. The reflections were all too real. You were only ever fighting with and
fishing for yourself.
But you still failed to see and again, kept fishing. About to drop 3 more nets,
and hope for something to stay in. Until finally, the girl at sea starts to
transform. Hard lessons. Even harder teachers. The girl at sea sails inward,
inland. She finds her own school of fish. Swimming through her toes, her
throat, swimming up her spine.

What are you fishing for, girl at sea?

You were born with everything you need.
You have always known that you are free.

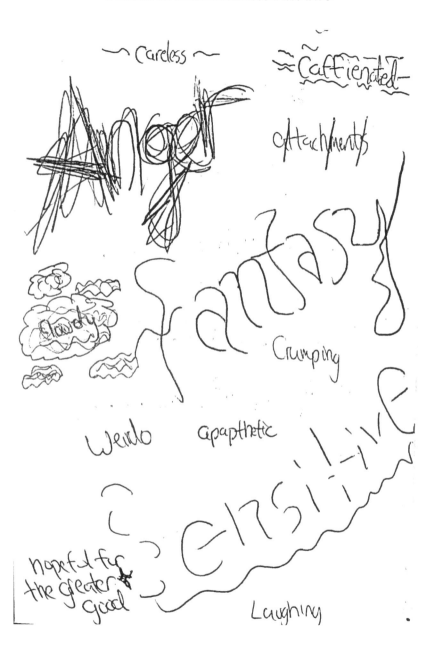

Careless

Caffienated

Angst

Attachments

Fantasy

Flawed

Crumping

Weird

Apapthetic

Sensitive

hopeful for the greater good

Laughing

Backyard Shed

When I was a little girl,
We used to build tents.

We would build tents
out of blankets
pillows
snow.
Little did we know
we were creating
little save havens
to be, just so.

When I was a little girl,
I used to wander.

I wandered under my shed.
The crisscross lattice
felt calming
over my head.
I'd sit, legs crossed
and feel safe
under the red outlined shed.

Smelling the smell of fresh cut grass.
Dad working hard in the yard.
Under the shed I would cast
my precious dreams, with no guard.

When I was a little girl,
I would dream.
I would go to dreamland
in my head
and become
a small woodland mammal
bringing peace to all channels
under the red outlined shed.

Foundation

"One Day At a Time"
you always told me.

From my first steps,
you challenged me
to be more than I was.

"Push harder, be better."

"You can't let your mood
be controlled by the weather."

Full of wisdom and words,
playing music from the soul;
you made our house a home,
foundation a whole.

"The road to success
is always under construction."
never once letting us
cause our own self-destruction.

You've built the four walls
that surrounded us five
from love, rises, and falls
together we thrive.

I'm grateful to know
that people like you
who take crap from so many
can hate so few.

I am with you.
You are with me.
You are my foundation.
Forever, that'll be.

The Higher Self

My entire being is unraveling.
These short split-second glimpses into my intuition don't make any sense.

Body awareness
feeling bones I didn't know
& centers lighting up
around different people.

Mental awareness
feeling pain I never had
& centers lighting up
around different emotions.

Ups
and
Downs.

Frustrations.

It is getting pretty heavy.

Old attachments.
Maybe
I want to hold
onto this
forever?

[I'm too proud of my ego.]

But it's getting unbearably heavy.
[I am scared of what is past my ego because it is all I know.]
It's forever too heavy.

So I learn to let it go.

I Took Back My Power

I took back my power today.
I took back my kindness.
I took back my confidence.
I took back my self-worth.
I took back my confidence.
I took back my confidence.
I took back my confidence.
I let go
and I took back my power today.

[I feel like this will never end]
[I feel like this is all my fault]
[Why can't I do anything right?]

I claim myself.
I took back my power today.

Walk Amongst

Can you walk amongst:
The fearful
The spiteful
The hateful
The shattered?

Can you walk amongst:
The drained
The burdened?
The blind
The battered?

Can you walk amongst:
The beautiful
The broken
The drunken
The outspoken?

Can you walk amongst:
The rough
The rude
The joyful
The prude?

Can you walk amongst:
The inspiring
The enlightened
The novel
The frightened?

If you Walk Amongst All,
surely you'll obtain
a silver seat in the sky
free from all chains.

Red Over Blue

Lucky are those who bleed outward, Red.
The inward blood is Blue.
Red, as it contacts the oxygenated, outside world.

My blood is Blue for you.

Hidden, inward, I've kept it in.
Flowing inside, deep Blue.

Yet nothing is more rusted than a voice Red with distrust.
But I do not hear Red voices.
I only see Red, anger and lust.
Blue with inward fear.

Sorry are those who think heaven is small.
Spectacled Blue sky above
blind to someone looking down
at the cracked and tainted pavement.

But for those who show the Red. The outward Red. For all to see.
Championed are those who see the Red.
The Red is the key.

I always preferred Red over Blue.

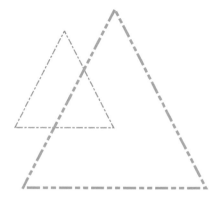

Ours

Your depths are inside my hands.
I feel you always.
You get it
without explanation;
telepathic communication.
Inside your depths,
I rest.

Resistance to none.
You leave, I feel whole.
Deeply protected and still.
"Rooted in love"
is our flow.
Will you permit my looking
into the soul of another?
I too, feel drawn to others.

My spirit is free;
untangled at last.
You
see my love
hear my truth
feel my scars.

This love,
in absence of others,
is ours.

Too Seriously

When my time comes
to shine
I take my SPF too seriously.

When my time comes
to dine
I take my veggies too seriously.

When my time comes
to love
I take my feelings too seriously.

When my time comes
to dance
I take my moves too seriously.

When my time comes
to talk
I take my words too seriously.

I forget I am free.

I am free to be me.

I do lots of things
to set myself free.

But I always forget
to stop and just be.

I simply take myself
too seriously.

A Skinned Heart

Rose-colored glasses
I see my world.
I wish I could afford
to be your girl.

Dance in the kitchen,
you let me twirl.
I wish I could afford
to be your girl.

I struggle with
the love within.
I want to skin my heart
can't win.

The way this goes,
it fails to flow.
It's all a show
'till someone goes
or you propose
a final act
to end the show.

The skinned heart shows
no steady blood flow
& all low blows.

My skinned heart chose
to love a dead rose.

My skinned heart rose
above the fake pose.

The skinned heart knows
death on The Row.

I Would Like to Share My Sky

Just because I would give you my Moon,
does not mean
you would give me your Sun.

Just because I would give you my Mercury,
does not mean
you would give me your mind.

Just because I would give you my Venus,
does not mean
you would give me your love.

Just because I would give you my Mars,
does not mean
you would give me your assertion.

Just because I would give you my Jupiter,
does not mean
you would give me your prosperity.

Just because I would give you my Saturn,
does not mean
you would give me your discipline.

Just because I would give you my Neptune,
does not mean
you would give me your dreams.

Just because I would give you my Uranus
does not mean
you would give me your eccentricity.

Just because I would give you my sky,
does not mean
you would give me your galaxy.

The Ascension Experience

We are vessels here to show each other our true selves. We are vessels here to heal with the exchange of creative energy.

We are not here to attach.

We do this to feel, integrating the physical with the spiritual.

We do not use our bodies. We value the body.

We ignite and align the body, so we can channel our highest states of bliss.

We do this to connect.

We do not do this for control, power, or ego.

We do not do this to fill a void.

We do this for vulnerability.

We do this for communion.

We do this to transmute our stagnant energy.

We do this to feel.

We do this to ascend.

Observation

Just simply observing.
The lost art.
Just simply using eyes to view.
No judgment.
No predictions.
No desirable outcomes.
No thoughts.

Everything is so instant now.
Everything feeds us.
What happened to just looking?

Pisces Moon

Most people choose
what is good for their situation.

Few people choose
what is good for their soul.

Cheer of The Year

Eight counts, spanks
bows and tights.
Pretty face.
"Look cheerful, my dear.
People depend on you for the light."
But what happens when the light
is artificial, unclear?
If you don't gossip
you don't fit in the mold.
If you don't praise your ego,
like you are told,
"Looks are gold!" in this game.
What happened to compassion?
Other friendships put on hold
for the sake of the squad.
I want to be free from this mold.
I want to tumble alone
while you gossip in your groups.
I know I was guilty, too.
But they never got me down.
They never took my crown.
Being me, I could see
through the pretty smiles

and their glistened lips,
glossed for daily gossip rounds.
I started to observe.
Stepped back and let them be.
Analyzed the white lies
& finally felt free
from the chains of the squad.
The competition, the disconnection
not with other teams
but with their own reflections.
I could see, that I too was competing
for my own inner perfection.
That artificial smile.
"But you did indeed feel yourself, some
while?"
Yes, under the spotlight,
every Friday night
when I tumbled down the track
to be met with my free-spirit
who just cannot be
a part of this pack.
This is not an attack.
They helped me love me.

I just hope now, that they too
are free.

Journal Page

Use this page to take notes on your individual truth.

My main ways I express myself creatively:

The tasks I need to take to get more in touch with my creativity:

My goals for my creations:

The Soul in the Land of the Blue

I met a soul.
I met a soul so beautiful
with just the same as me.
Looks fine in a sweater,
no matter the weather.
and silly as can be.

I met a soul.
So kind and true.
A radiance of love anew.
This soul is tainted,
now this is true.
That's why they're here, in the Land of the Blue.

I met a soul.
Just like my own.
So happy-go-lucky
that I too own.
This soul is funny, kind, and sweet.
Can't help but say,
swept off my feet.

I met this soul.
and I dare say,
I love this soul
on this fine day.

I love this soul, forever more.
I see my future,
the past ashore.

I see this soul.
so deep and through.
I'm glad they're here, in the Land of the Blue.

Blue Little Lives [The Pleiades]

My sky failed to realize
as much as I tried.
I missed
the Who,
the What,
the Where,
the How,
and always
the Why.

I got so caught up in the path's little lies.
The Tricks,
the Turns,
the Trials,
the Compromise.

I got lost along the way
to the channel of skies.
I got too caught up in those sparkling eyes.
the Denial,
the Defeat,
drew me to
the Demise.

I suppose I'll go back to my
blue little lives.

Process to Progress

I am water.
I am deep and vast.
I lay down and cry,
feel, surrender
always for a greater good.
I process
so I can progress.

Emotions, she runs so deep
yet she strives for all to see.
I process
so I can progress.

It may look wild
yet her soul is just that.
Wild and free,
beautiful blooming lily.
I process
so I can progress.

In time, pain subsides.
I do not store fear.
I process
so I can progress.

I progress far and near.

Neptune in Nature

Neptune represents illusions and all that is unclear.
...But I let go of my fear.

I release all hurts
about life
about love
about future illusions
and past Neptune's too.

With rose-colored glasses
the gas giant Neptune
gives us passes
to dream.

My life is my illusion
I write to stop confusion.
I love it all.
I create my own conclusions.
My creation is my resolution.
My delusion is my union.

I embrace my own start.
Pent up anger and fear
will release
at the gates
of my own heart.

I only allow joyous
positive thoughts
even if they are
Neptune in nature.

A Strong Woman

To sum it up, these were my takeaways from her:

You cannot wish your life away.
You cannot wish your life to be a certain way.
You have got to know right from wrong.
You have got to make decisions.
You have got to have some sort of income coming in.
You have got to let your emotions take a back seat sometimes.
Be grateful for what you already have.
The sun will come out tomorrow.
Whatever will be, will be.
Luv ya to the moon.
Wear perfume. Tea tree oil is too pungent a smell.

Steeler Sunday

The energy
of a Steeler Sunday
is unmatched, unrivaled,
undefeated.

Seeing the auras of those around me
light up.

Smile
cheer
get happy
get pissed off
get nervous
get anxious
get excited
get sad
is why I love these days.

Seeing people express
no sense of responsibilities.
Putting life down for a day
for the sake of the Steel Curtain.

Betting and competing with opinions and the feelings
that encompass the space around the arena
and the big screen garage TV.

This is a fine Steeler Sunday to me.

Anyway

I don't like that side of me,
but I love me anyway.

I don't like my passiveness,
but I love me anyway.

I don't like my vulnerability,
but I love me anyway.

I don't like my attitude,
but I love me anyway.

I don't like my need to escape,
but I love me anyway.

I don't like my endless thoughts,
but I love me anyway.

I don't like my need for answers,
but I love me anyway.

I don't really like you,
but I love you anyway.

Dante

You are here
little cadet from space.
I think we might
be from the same place.

Beep Boop Boop Bop
You're the cutest
little tot
and I want you to know
there's no mission
you can't face.

It's nice here on Earth
we have
objects
gadgets
and
gizmos.

I see you too,
look up high
to the Cosmos.

Little buddy,
I love you
and I'm so
glad you're here.

Earth is fun
Let's go run
on this
ever moving Sphere.

Creation

Creation is everything.
We have infinite power to create through our words and actions.
When we suppress our creative nature, we sometimes unknowingly
express judgment of self and others' unique creations.

Let your creative forces flow through you and speak to you.
Or keep your creations inward.

Your truest self speaks through your creations.
Embrace creativity.
Spread new seeds to inspire new growth.

Fragments of Lust

Shaping fragments of lust
into love
take trust.

Lust is cold.
Love is fever.

Words are weak
when actions don't speak either.

Light Beings are Coming to Earth

I was afraid what might come up
if I took up writing as a thing.
But it's the deepest part of me,
and its dying to sing.

I was afraid what might pop up
if I took to a life of healing.
Vibing too hard with my toxic health,
but really I was stealing
myself from me.
How could that even be?
Vibing with the toxic self,
 'till I saw the self eternally.

I thought that I had figured out
but I am being reborn.
People need to fall away
to make room for more.

Light beings are ascending fast.
Incarnating at light speeds;
faster than a spinning glass
and all these new-age "techy" feeds.

So, what do I do here, on this Earth plane?
I write, I be, I show, I love,
I connect to the sky above,
I have heart for the lame.
Some missions are complete
with beings of the past.
The key is to accept it,
but know it always lasts.

We live on together,
yes you, and also me.
So why you questioning forever?

Light beings are coming to Earth, eternally.

Sell My Worries

The strength of my shell
is not determined by
the length of my worries.

I fell.

Too much in a hurry;
day after day
trying not to swell
up with flurries
of fear
that spread through my being.

I started to
sell my worries
& it was freeing.

Boxing Gloves

Scattered spectacles of her doubts
live in her mind.
A salient memory
of a down-and-out time
still lives there.
Buried in the mind-mine,
she chooses to rise above the grime,
chooses the boxing gloves
and fights for the light
that she elected to ignore
for such a long plight.
Yet today, her thoughts,
she can adore.

Woke Up on a Roof

I Woke Up on a roof
in the cold air
with a cold beer
and you.

I mean "Woke Up",
as in "no longer aloof"
to the world and all
I knew to be so true.

I don't know if you noticed
'cause our egos were busy
talking about
all our troubles
and all our miseries.

You would ask why I laugh
and I'd say 'cause of you.

You were there to listen
to my outspoken intuition,
and to my mystic mind.
My eyes, they glisten
and you knew I was wishin'
to find one of my cryptic kind.
But we, my love, are intertwined.

So, that's when
I Woke Up
on a roof
in the cold air
with a cold beer
and
you.

Smoke Always Rises

Stabilize the heat inside of you.
She starts to feel through
the heat she's created.

"You've made your own pain."
Jaded,
she tries to extinguish the flame;
tries to distinguish love from pain.

She improvises.

But she too knows.
And she too plays the game.

But smoke always rises.

Re-Set

I've left my claws, with love,
in the past.

Claws of the past
no long press into my skin's nodes.
Flowers of the future
no longer flood my frontal lobe.
Capacity to compassionately create
is creeping into the crevices of my crown.
The dead energy passed on.
Transmuted into hoops and heaps of hope.
I want to express nothing less than my soul.
Regress to past breaths I've taken unfold.
Brightness of the future, no longer cold or untrue.
The colors align, vibrations of my inner mind feel anew.
Grateful for the darkness, yet welcoming the shine.
This kind of emotion is ever divine.
I bathe and I breathe, my cells recharge.
For days, I dream of endless regards;
love, hope, unity, and freedom at last

I've left my claws, with love,
in the past.

Deduction: Be You

It is always better to
just
be
you
than to be
what
you might think
you might be.

We are all the truth.

No one truly knows what to do.

No one truly knows the truth.

We all come to know our own truth.

Let's just promise
to see
each other through.

When it's all said and done
We all come undone.
No more daydream runs.
This was all just for fun.

I promise to you, this will hold true
I will now just simply be me
and you can just simply be
you, however true to you
you want to do
I see you
Be you
too.

Seen Through

Liquid drop in a bucket.
Skinny vein in a leaf.
Golden ember in a fire.
Broken heart in a thief.

Some things are so brief;
so fleeting, so small.

Some things mean nothing;
broken clock on a wall.

Written note in a pool,
black ink bleeding, diffuse.
Hard truth in a lie,
hearts feeling misused.

Some things are so clear
so heard, seen through.

Some things are so deep.
Him looking at you.

The Seeker Not in Vain

He does not hide behind
the stage in hard times.

He wears his pain.
He shows his stains.
When he is close to the cliff,
he skins his knees
and other climbers see.
He is not afraid
to show his pain.
He is raw.
He is untamed.
Whatever the task,
he brings the lion's mane.
Roars into the Earth
a new way to do.
He never commits
without seeing it through.
Every word he speaks,
every act he takes
in these hard times
undoubtedly show
he wears his pain.
Painted on a canvas called skin.
Faithful to the journey towards love.
His angel is on Earth; no longer above.
In these times, he does not grow weaker.
He, The Seeker,
does not live in vain.

The Last Fighter Jet

The last Fighter Jet zoomed off the runway. Carrying the grounded energy amidst aiming to be in the clouds. The pilot was a 27-year-old newly licensed lad who embraced the structure of a flight fighter from the Vietnam era, yet embodied a futuristic and innovative nature.
Growing up, the young pilot knew his purpose.
He was destined to fly high.
Destined to be above the physical plane.

Private school did not serve him as a young lad. Being such an innovator and a creative force, he didn't stand a chance with the jocks and the letterman's.

Young flighty man had his thoughts in the clouds.

Dreaming of the architectural structures of the jets, at top speeds of 437 mph with a 39' wingspan and a state-of-the art V12 Packard Rolls Royce Merlin engine, flight man knew his calling.
He had the gusto and the etiquette fit for the cabin.
He had impeccable control system management and an innate knowing of all the air had to offer from a young age.
"You dream too big, lad." Mama would chirp in his ear.

"We're workin' folk, Anderson, we tend to the land, not the clouds.

Ain't nothin' up there for us."
But these jabs were always in one ear and out the other.
Flight man was destined to soar.
Now, I sit and watch him take off from my patio table at the restaurant in Georgia.
A true Southern Boy in the sun, breaking free from the "simple plan".

I can hear the co-pilot chirping in his ear, "Easy now, boy. You done did as well on your license test but you ain't mastered the sky yet. Keep those dreams of yours on the ground, boy. Ain't no pilot ever find his way up here all a' once."

"I'm a workin' folk." Replied the flight man.
"I tend to the clouds, not the land."

When I Love You

You will know when I love you. It's the way I'll look at you when you aren't looking at me. You won't see it, but you will know what it looks like.
When I love you, I will want to hug you all the time.
When I love you, I will say one thing, and do the other.
I will act like what's behind my eyes isn't an intense pool of emotion that longs to pour into you.
When I love you, I will do my own thing. I will go my own way.
I might even leave.
But I will always come back,
because my spirit will feel so free, that it can roam and explore.
Because I will feel whole in your love.
I might even disappear.
But I will always come back.
I might need to re-balance myself.
I might need to take a solo walk, get some air,
because you always have a way of stealing my breath.
When I love you, I will fight for you.
When I love you, I will fight with you.
I might tell you "I don't trust you",
only because I might feel, at that time, like I don't trust my own heart.
But I trust you to love me. Wholly. Unconditionally.
When I love you, I will go into that space in my mind that I dare not ever go because I will feel supported with you next to me.
I will feel safe in your darkness, and you in mine.
When I love you, I will make you sad.
I will make you angry, I might make you mad
because when I love you, you will feel everything.
I will show you yourself, when I love you.
When I love you, I will squeeze you so hard, hold you so tight. Tense and tight love.
When I love you, I will love everyone because you make me want to spread my heart to the world. You make me want to show myself. Unconditionally.
When I love you, you will know you're the only one I love in this way.
When I love you, it might be intense, childlike, contradicting, spacey, back-and-forth, push and pull, heart-opening, confusing, yet FREE.
When I love you, I will see you for the opposite, closed, broken, beautiful mess that you are . . . .

because that mess is me, too.

Gina Louise Angela Della Valle

Gina, or GLAD, is a 27-year-old blooming writer. Despite her full initials being GLAD, Gina's writing style often showcase emotional rawness and inner wounding. Gina threads together esoteric notes and lines of truth within her writing. She displays both broken and healed free-verse lines of uncomfortable soul-level realizations and boundless self-love. Gina's writing purpose is to unapologetically break the chains of toxic positivity. She unveils the reality and superpowers behind being a woman with deep emotion. In hopes for a paradigm shift in the way humans relate to one another, Gina believes in cutting through the societal norms of what has become an overly materialistic and emotionally suppressive world. Words serve as medicine for the soul. Gina's writing connects all readers to the eternal spirit of life. Write to me at gdella3313@yahoo.com Connect with me on
Gdella3313@yahoo.com
Youtube: GinaDellaValle

Marisa Camille Berkey

grew up in a military family and moved to different areas her whole life. She has a very loving and close relationship with her family. They always keep her spirits up and support her creative ideas.

Marisa first found herself when she was living in Hawaii and experienced the *Aloha* culture. She fell in love with the people and how beautiful the island was. At this point in her young age, she knew this State was going to make a large impact on her life.

After leaving Hawaii, Marisa continued to use her *Aloha* influence everywhere she went. She loves to create floral designs with vibrant colors and positive energy. She enjoys brightening people's days and creating strong bonds through art. Marisa is a Gemini who is open to expressing her passion and excited to start this journey with Gina.

Lightning Source UK Ltd.
Milton Keynes UK
UKHW021452080922
408530UK00005B/168

9 798210 607515